AGS

Basic English Composition
Student Workbook

by
Bonnie L. Walker

American Guidance Service, Inc.
Circle Pines, Minnesota 55014-1796
800-328-2560

Printed in the United States of America

ISBN 0-7854-0541-0

Product Number 90033

A 0 9 8 7

Table of Contents

Finding Sentences

Directions:
- Read each group of words below.
- Find the sentences and list them in order.
- Capitalize the first word in each sentence.
- Put a punctuation mark at the end.

EXAMPLE   everyone in my family likes ice cream our favorite flavor is chocolate we often have ice cream for dessert

1) Everyone in my family likes ice cream.
2) Our favorite flavor is chocolate.
3) We often have ice cream for dessert.

---

1) in the spring we planted a garden we planted cabbages and peas first later we planted tomatoes

2) my aunt sent me a book for my birthday I wrote a letter to thank her she was pleased

3) my friends and I started a band we practiced three times a week soon we sounded very good

4) last night it snowed again the streets were slippery this morning we looked in the garage for our sleds

5) there was an ad in the newspaper for a file clerk the person had to put papers in alphabetic order I decided to apply for the job

6) yesterday my sister went to the library she wanted to find a book about guitars her music teacher told the class to write a report about a musical instrument

7) today there was an announcement on the public address system at school the coach is having tryouts for the basketball team my friend and I decided to go

8) every year the senior class produces a play usually it is a musical we have a lot of talent at our school

9) what two things must a writer always do a writer must capitalize the first work of a sentence he or she also must put a punctuation mark at the end

Expressing Ideas

The same idea can be expressed with the same words in different ways. The words of a sentence can be placed in a different order.

EXAMPLE   Every year the family usually goes camping.

The family usually goes camping every year.

Usually the family goes camping every year.

Directions: Rewrite each sentence below. Change the words around. Find a different word in the sentence to put at the beginning. Capitalize the first word. Remember end punctuation.

1) We seldom watch television in the summer.

_____

2) We are usually too busy with outdoor activities.

_____

3) Always the weather is sunny and warm where we live.

_____

4) Lately we have not had much rain in our town.

_____

5) Suddenly I heard thunder rumbling in the background.

_____

6) Everyone immediately was sure that we would have rain.

_____

7) In a few minutes the thunder stopped.

_____

8) Slowly we opened the door and looked outside.

_____

9) At that moment the sky was clear as far as we could see.

_____

10) Someday soon, I'm sure, we finally will get some rain.

_____

Writing in Sentences

Directions: Answer each question by writing a complete sentence.
Capitalize the first word in each sentence. Put a
punctuation mark at the end.

EXAMPLE	What is your favorite holiday?

My favorite holiday is Christmas.

1) What is today's date?

_____

_____

2) What is your name?

_____

_____

3) How old are you?

_____

_____

4) In which state do you live?

_____

_____

5) What is the capital city of your state?

_____

_____

6) Who is president of the United States?

_____

_____

7) What is your favorite color?

_____

_____

8) Do you have cable television in your
community?

_____

_____

9) What is the name of your teacher?

_____

_____

10) Which is your favorite sport or hobby?

_____

_____

11) Who is your favorite singer?

_____

_____

12) What is the name of the last movie you saw?

_____

_____

13) Did you enjoy the movie?

_____

_____

What's the Purpose?

Directions: On the line before each sentence write the purpose of the
sentence. Then add the correct end punctuation mark.

Statement	To give information
Question	To ask for information
Command	To tell someone to do something
Exclamation	To express strong feelings

1) _____ Having a bank account is important

2) _____ What kind of bank account do you have

3) _____ Laura asked, "Can you have more than one type of account"

4) _____ "Oh, sure you can," replied Amanda

5) _____ Derek exclaimed, "I have enough money to buy a stereo"

6) _____ Laura explained that she has just opened her account

7) _____ Amanda said, "I am saving to buy a car when I graduate"

8) _____ Derek then asked, "What are you saving for, Laura"

9) _____ "I don't know," said Laura

10) _____ Derek yelled, "You should know"

11) _____ "Leave her alone," ordered Amanda

12) _____ Mrs. Lewis has two accounts

13) _____ Does she have a checking account

14) _____ She has a checking account with a large bank

15) _____ Amanda asked, "What is the purpose of a checking account"

16) _____ Laura explained, "You use a checking account in place of cash"

17) _____ Derek exclaimed, "It is safer than cash"

18) _____ Laura laughed, "Derek, write me a check"

19) _____ How do you choose the correct bank

20) _____ You must do research before choosing a bank

The Purpose of a Sentence

Directions: Read each sentence. Decide what its purpose is. Add the
correct end punctuation marks. Write the correct letter
before each sentence.

  A. To make a statement.
  B. To ask a question.
  C. To give a command or make a request.
  D. To express strong feeling.

_____ **1)** Have you every read *The Red Pony*

_____ **2)** It is a story by John Steinbeck

_____ **3)** What a wonderful story it is

_____ **4)** *The Red Pony* was written in 1933

_____ **5)** Read it for your next book report

_____ **6)** *The Red Pony* is still a popular book

_____ **7)** Maybe that is because it is so short

_____ **8)** *The Red Pony* is a heartwarming story

_____ **9)** Have you ever seen the movie

_____ **10)** The main character is a ten-year-old boy named Jody

_____ **11)** Remember that name

_____ **12)** His father was very stern

_____ **13)** He gave Jody a red pony to take care of

_____ **14)** "Feed him and clean him every day"

_____ **15)** The pony's name was Gabilan

_____ **16)** At first he was scared and wild

_____ **17)** Gabilan and Jody became friends

_____ **18)** How Jody loved that pony

_____ **19)** Do you want to know what happened next

_____ **20)** Read the book and find the answer

Punctuating Dialogue

Directions: Here are some sentences with dialogue. Add quotation marks, commas, and end punctuation marks where they are needed.

Plans for Camping

1) Let's go camping next weekend Mike suggested

2) That sounds good to me Derek agreed

3) I have a tent. Do you have any equipment Mike asked

4) Well said Derek I have a sleeping bag

5) What about a stove asked Mike

6) Derek thought for a while. Then he said I think that I can borrow one from my boss

7) Then Mike's little brother Tim came in and asked Can I go, too

8) Mike looked at Derek and smiled. Sure, you can go

9) We will hike about ten miles before we make camp Mike said

10) Derek added Then we'll catch fish for our dinner

11) At night we will curl up inside our sleeping bags said Mike We'll be warm inside the tent

12) That will be fun laughed Tim We will have a great time

13) Do you think we'll see any bears this year asked Derek

14) No chance said Mike We almost never see a bear up there

15) Anyway, they are always friendly said Derek

16) I just remembered something Tim said

17) Mike looked at his brother. What is that, Tim

18) I think I have a baseball game this weekend he said

19) Too bad said Derek. It would have been fun

20) Sure, guys said Tim but maybe next time

Who's Speaking Now?

Dialogue is conversation. A quotation is the exact words that
someone says.

Start a new paragraph each time a different person speaks.

EXAMPLE	"I'm looking for my friend, Nathan," Janet said. "Have you seen him?"
	Carol thought for a minute. Then she said, "Yes, I think I saw him at the library."

Directions: Rewrite the following paragraph. Punctuate the dialogue
correctly. Start a new paragraph when a different person
speaks.

The Playoffs
Everyone met at Whitemarsh Park at 6:30 P.M. "Hey,
Coach," called Clark. "What time does the game start?"
The coach looked at the schedule. "It says here the game
starts at 6:45 P.M. Take a turn at bat and then get out in
the field. Be sure to warm up thoroughly." "Sure thing,
Coach," Clark smiled and picked up his favorite bat. Soon
the game got under way. "Batter up," the umpire yelled.

_____

_____

_____

_____

_____

_____

_____

_____

_____

_____

Direct and Indirect Quotations

Direct: "I like a cup of hot tea in the morning," said Jan.
Indirect: Jan said that she liked a cup of hot tea in the morning.

A. Directions: Change each of these indirect quotations to a direct
quotation. Punctuate and capitalize each sentence correctly.

1) Karen asked Fred if he wanted a second piece of cake.

2) Fred reminded her that he was trying to maintain his weight.

3) Karen laughed and said he should have told her sooner.

4) She said she could have given him an apple for dessert.

5) Fred said that he'd rather have cake.

B. Directions: Now change these direct quotations to indirect quotations.
Do not use quotation marks. Be sure to punctuate
correctly.

1) "Sit down and have a good breakfast," Harold's father said.

2) "Breakfast is the most important meal of the day," he continued.

3) Harold shrugged, "But I'm in a hurry, Dad."

4) "Besides," Harold said, "I'm not hungry in the morning."

5) "I won't take no for an answer, Son." Harold's father was firm.

Making Your Subject and Verb Agree

A singular subject needs a singular verb form.

A plural subject needs a plural verb form.

EXAMPLES   Singular subject — One **girl** walks home.

Plural subject — Many **girls** walk home.

Directions: The subject of each of these sentences is in bold print. The verbs are in parentheses. Complete each sentence by writing the correct form of the verb on the line.

1) **Both** of my friends _____ going to the party. (is, are)

2) **Carolyn** _____ a party every year. (gives, give)

3) **She** _____ the best snacks you ever tasted.

    (makes, make)

4) **Carolyn** _____ a recreation room in her basement.

    (has, have)

5) **Her mother and father** _____ upstairs. (stays, stay)

6) **Carolyn** usually _____ Fred for her date.

    (invites, invite)

7) **He and Carolyn** _____ parties. (loves, love)

8) **They** both _____ to eat. (likes, like)

9) **Fred** always _____ there early. (gets, get)

10) **Everyone** _____ that they'd better come on time or

    there may be nothing left! (knows, know)

11) Carolyn's **father** always _____ the same thing. (does, do)

12) There _____ a large **clock** on the wall. (is, are)

13) Her **dad** always _____ downstairs about midnight. (comes, come)

14) He checks to be sure the **clock** still _____. (works, work)

Using Pronouns

A pronoun must agree in number and gender with the word it replaces.

EXAMPLES	Where did **Mary** go? (singular, feminine noun)

Where did **she** go?

Nancy and Joanie are sisters. (plural)

They are sisters.

Directions: Change the bold noun to a pronoun in each of these sentences.
Write the new sentence on the lines.

1) **Sam and Eleanor** agreed to meet for lunch.

_____

_____

2) Sam planned to meet Eleanor after **Eleanor's** French class.

_____

_____

3) **Eleanor's** French teacher is Mrs. Bernstein.

_____

_____

4) Mrs. Bernstein had given **Mrs. Bernstein's** class a long assignment.

_____

_____

5) Eleanor didn't understand **the assignment** completely.

_____

_____

6) **Eleanor** was still talking to Mrs. Bernstein about it when Sam arrived.

_____

_____

7) Sam paced back and forth because Eleanor was making **Eleanor and Sam** late for lunch.

_____

_____

8) Finally **Eleanor** came out of the classroom.

_____

_____

9) "**Eleanor** is sorry to keep you waiting," Eleanor said.

_____

_____

10) "OK, but let's hurry. The special today is spaghetti, and I don't want to miss **the spaghetti**," said Sam.

_____

_____

Capitalization of Proper Nouns

• A proper noun is the name of a particular person, place, thing, or idea.
• Always capitalize proper nouns in sentences.

Activity 1:
Write a proper noun beside each common noun.

EXAMPLE	television	*Zenith*

1) state _____

2) city _____

3) movie _____

4) book _____

5) song _____

6) continent _____

7) ocean _____

8) friend _____

9) school _____

10) river _____

11) restaurant _____

12) food store _____

13) special event _____

14) university _____

15) airline _____

16) cereal _____

17) soft drink _____

18) month _____

19) holiday _____

20) religion _____

Activity 2:
What does each proper noun below name? Write the correct common noun.

EXAMPLE	Labor Day	*holiday*

1) Algebra II _____

2) French _____

3) December _____

4) Junior Prom _____

5) Ritz Theater _____

6) *The Sound of Music* _____

7) the Indian Ocean _____

8) the Rocky Mountains _____

9) San Francisco _____

10) West Virginia _____

11) the Ford Building _____

12) Andrew Jackson _____

13) South America _____

14) Lake Erie _____

15) Stanford University _____

16) Julia Roberts _____

17) *Lassie Come Home* _____

18) Chicago _____

19) William Shakespeare _____

20) the Middle East _____

Plurals and Possessives

A. Directions: Look at each noun in bold print. Decide whether it is singular or plural. Look for the word in the list below the sentences. Beside the word write **S** for Singular or **P** for Plural.

1) One **day** Mrs. **O'Hara** got a **letter** in the **mail**.

2) The **letter** said that she had jury **duty**.

3) A **jury** is a **group** of twelve **people**

4) Its **members** listen to **evidence**.

5) They judge the defendant's **guilt** or **innocence**.

6) All twelve **men** and **women** must agree.

1) day _____   3) jury _____   5) guilt _____

   Mrs. O'Hara _____   group _____   innocence _____

   letter _____   people _____   6) men _____

   mail _____   4) members _____   women _____

2) letter _____   evidence _____

   duty _____

B. Directions: The apostrophes have been left out of the phrases below. Read each phrase. If it has a possessive noun, write the phrase on the line. Put an apostrophe in the correct place.

| **EXAMPLES** | the lady's hat (singular possessive) |
| | the ladies' club; the men's club (plural possessives) |

---

1) the wolfs howl _____   6) your two cents worth _____

2) the calves pen _____   7) a days pay _____

3) all of the teams _____   8) two weeks a year _____

4) the childrens room _____   9) the familys home _____

5) the students book _____   10) the cars tire _____

Make Them Correct

Directions: Each of these sentences has a mistake. Find the error and circle it. Write the sentence correctly.

1) Amanda and Laura works together.

   _____

   _____

2) They work at a Restaurant.

   _____

3) They are work as waitresses.

   _____

   _____

4) "I glad that we only work until six o'clock today," said Laura.

   _____

   _____

5) "Do you has a date tonight?" asked Amanda.

   _____

   _____

6) "Yes, I am go to a movie with Bill," replied Laura.

   _____

   _____

7) "Bills father is lending us the car," Laura explained.

   _____

   _____

8) "I is going out with some of Derek's friends," said Amanda.

   _____

   _____

9) After Laura worked her shift, she goes home.

   _____

   _____

10) At home Laura eated dinner.

    _____

    _____

11) She went to her room and gets ready for her date.

    _____

    _____

12) Laura buyed a new outfit for the date.

    _____

    _____

13) When Laura went downstairs, she looks beautiful.

    _____

    _____

14) Bill sayed, "Laura, you look great!"

    _____

    _____

15) As they leaved, Laura's mother called, "Don't be late!"

    _____

    _____

Homonyms

Here are some homonyms that we often use in our everyday writing. Read the definitions and examples carefully. Then do the exercises.

A.   **right** (rit) *adjective* — related to the side of the body that is away from the heart.

right (rit) *adjective* — correct, true.

write (rit) *verb* — to form letters and words with a pen or pencil on a piece of paper.

| EXAMPLES | Your answer to the question was **right**.
Please **write** your answer on this paper. |

Directions: Read each sentence. Then write either *right* or *write* in the space.

1) When are you planning to _____ your aunt a letter?

2) Give me the _____ answer to the question.

3) Most people _____ with their _____ hand.

4) Derek looked left and _____ before he crossed the road.

5) Mike forgot to _____ his name on his test paper.

B.   **which** (wich) *pronoun* — what one of a group of things; used to introduce a clause.

witch (wich) *noun* — a woman who is said to practice evil magic.

| EXAMPLES | **Which** of those books did you like best?
The wicked **witch** gave Snow White a poison apple. |

Directions: Write *which* or *witch* in each space.

1) Amanda didn't know _____ shoes to buy.

2) There was a very mean _____ in the *Wizard of Oz*.

3) _____ of those roasts looks bigger?

4) Shirley went to the party dressed as a _____

5) Laura lifted weights, _____ kept her in good condition.

Confusing Words

A. Here are three words that all sound alike. Their meanings are quite different!

> **pear** *noun* — a fruit
>
> **pair** *noun* — two things that go together
>
> **pare** *verb* — to peel; to cut off the outer layer

EXAMPLES	Our **pear** tree is loaded with fruit.

Amanda decided which **pair** of shoes she wanted.

Mrs. O'Hara will **pare** the apples before she cooks them.

Directions: Write *pear*, *pair*, or *pare* on the blank line to make each sentence correct. You may make the word plural.

1) Are you going to _____ the _____ today?

2) The _____ become ripe in August every year.

3) Amanda and Laura are quite a _____ .

4) Please _____ these potatoes for dinner.

5) Derek needed a new _____ of track shoes.

B. Here are two more words that we use quite often.

> **course** *noun* — a path or route; a program of study.
>
> **coarse** *adjective* — rough; not smooth.

EXAMPLES	Your English **course** is very important.

The **course** of the river was winding.

The cloth was very **coarse**.

Directions: Write *course* or *coarse* on the blank line to make each sentence correct.

1) Do you have a golf _____ near your home?

2) Sometimes wool can be very _____ .

3) We followed the _____ of the river to its mouth.

4) The path through the woods was _____ .

5) Mrs. Gonzalez signed up for a swimming _____ .

Sound-Alike Words

A. Here are three little words that give people trouble!

> **buy** *verb* — to purchase.
>
> **bye** *interjection* — part of the expression "good-bye."
>
> **bye** *noun* — in a tournament, a round in which a player is not paired with an opponent and wins automatically.
>
> **by** *preposition* — near to or next to something.

EXAMPLES	
	Mike decided to **buy** a new tennis racket.
	"I'm leaving. **Bye**, now," said Laura.
	In the tennis tournament, Mike got a **bye** on the first round.
	Derek lives in the house **by** the park.

Directions: Write *buy*, *bye*, or *by* in each blank to make the sentence correct.

1) Ms. Lentz wanted to _____ a house _____ the lake.

2) "I got a _____ in the tournament," said Mike.

3) "When you leave, be sure to say _____," said Amanda.

4) The gas station was _____ a busy shopping center.

B. Homonyms are words that we must think about before we spell them. Here are three more words that sound exactly alike.

> **I'll** — a contraction for *I will*.
>
> **aisle** *noun* — a path between two parts of something.
>
> **isle** *noun* — a small island

EXAMPLES	
	I'll see you later.
	Mike walked slowly down the **aisle** at the movies, looking for a seat.
	Have you ever heard of the **Isle** of Capri?

Directions: Write *I'll*, *aisle*, or *isle* in each blank to make the sentence correct.

1) The survivors of the shipwreck lived on the _____ .

2) Between each row of desks was a narrow _____ .

3) Please pick up the paper in the _____ next to you.

4) "_____ probably be back in an hour," said Mike.

Words That Sound Alike

Here is a pair of especially tricky words: **desert** and **dessert**. The word *desert* has two pronunciations and two different meanings. One pronunciation sounds exactly like *dessert*. Read the definitions and examples below carefully.

desert (dez'-ərt) *noun* — dry, arid stretch of land.

desert (di-zert') *verb* — to leave without planning to return.

dessert (di-zert') *noun* — the last course of a meal; usually something sweet.

A tall cactus
grew in the
desert.

The mice decided
to **desert** the
barn.

Tim's favorite
dessert is ice cream!

Directions: Read each sentence carefully. Write either *desert* or *dessert* in the space.

1) What would you like tonight for _____ ?

2) I wouldn't want to be lost in the Sahara _____ .

3) There is a _____ in Arizona. Have you been there?

4) I hope you won't _____ me if I need help!

5) Fruit makes a good _____ .

6) A captain must never _____ the ship.

7) After the main course, people sometimes have _____ .

8) The faithful dog would not _____ his master.

9) Amanda's favorite _____ is chocolate pudding.

10) If you are crossing a _____ , take plenty of water!

Little Words, Big Trouble

A possessive noun needs an apostrophe. A possessive pronoun does not. Remember that fact to avoid making the most common spelling errors.

Also, remember that contractions need apostrophes to show that letters have been left out.

Its and It's

Possessive Pronoun: ——→ **Its** toy is broken

Contraction for *it is*: ——→ **It's** a lovely day.

There, Their, They're

Adverb: ——→ **There** goes a Mercedes!

Possessive Pronoun: ——→ **Their** phone is ringing.

Contraction for *they are*: ——→ **They're** very nice.

Directions   Complete each sentence. Circle the correct word in parentheses. Then write it on the line.

1) The baby is crying. I think _____ hungry. (it's, its)

2) Where is_____ mother? (it's, its)

3) What is _____ name, I wonder? (it's, its)

4) That must be her over _____ . (there, their, they're)

5) The mother and father are coming this way. _____ probably leaving. (There, Their, They're)

6) Look, _____ chauffeur is waiting for them. (there, their, they're)

7) You're kidding! _____ not possible. (It's, Its)

8) Well, he's holding _____ door open for them. (there, their, they're)

9) Wow! _____ really a chauffeur! (It's, Its)

10) _____ car is terrific. Is that a Rolls Royce? (Their, They're, There)

11) Is _____ color purple or maroon? (it's, its)

12) I'm not sure, but I know _____ pulling away. (it's, its)

A Camping Trip

Directions: Find the spelling errors in this story and circle them.
Write the words correctly on the lines below each sentence.

1) David and Robert are going on a camping

   trip Wensday.

   _____

   _____

2) They are excited becuse the whether is

   supposed two be good.

   _____

   _____

3) They got all of there supplys together.

   _____

   _____

4) David bought close and other things

   at the store.

   _____

   _____

5) Robert packed too sleeping bags and a tent.

   _____

   _____

6) The boys' parents will drive them too the

   camp were they were staying.

   _____

   _____

7) Robert said, "Let's go two bed now. I know

   you want to get up too hours before dawn."

   _____

   _____

8) The boys where awake early the next moring.

   _____

   _____

9) Father asked, "Do you have everything

   neccessary four you're trip?"

   _____

   _____

10) Both boys replied, "Were ready to go!"

    _____

    _____

11) The boys were gone fore one weak.

    _____

    _____

12) They had a terrific experience.

    _____

    _____

13) They hiked threw the mountains and

    swam in a lake.

    _____

    _____

14) "Did you sea any wild animals?" asked Mother.

    _____

    _____

15) "Wonc we saw rabbits and squirrels,"

    laughed David.

    _____

    _____

Avoiding the Comma Fault

A **comma fault** is using a comma by itself to connect or separate two ideas.
- At the end of a sentence, you must use *end punctuation*.
- Never use a comma to end a sentence.
- Never use a comma by itself to connect two sentences.

> *Wrong:* Carolyn is giving a party, we are all going.
>
> *Right:* Carolyn is giving a party, **and** we are all going.
>
> *Right:* Carolyn is giving a party. We are all going.

Commas may be used to separate words in a series.

> *Right:* Victor, Mike, and Tina rode in a helicopter.
>
> *Right:* Victor liked the ride a little, Mike didn't like it at all,
>
> and Tina now plans to become a pilot.

Directions: Rewrite these sentences. Correct any errors.

1) Helicopters are fun to ride in, they are also scary.

_____

_____

2) On her first ride Tina fell in love with flying, now she wants to be a pilot.

_____

_____

_____

3) Victor thought flying was OK, Mike made plans to take a bus next time.

_____

_____

_____

4) The fastest a helicopter ever flew was over 200 miles per hour, the pilot was Byron Graham.

_____

_____

_____

5) Byron Graham isn't in the National Aviation Hall of Fame, the Hall of Fame is in Dayton, Ohio, it honors outstanding pioneers.

_____

_____

_____

_____

_____

6) Some of the people in the Hall of Fame are Amelia Earhart, Wiley Post, Orville and Wilbur Wright, also in the Hall of Fame are Charles Lindbergh, and Alexander Graham Bell.

_____

_____

_____

_____

_____

_____

_____

Separating the Ideas

Directions: Each group of words below contains several sentences.
You must decide where each sentence begins and ends.
Rewrite the sentences correctly. Add the correct
punctuation.

The Labrador Retriever
The Wilsons got a labrador retriever puppy it was eight weeks old
and weighed ten pounds by the time it was three months old the
puppy weighed over thirty pounds the veterinarian said the puppy
might be over one hundred pounds when he was full-grown Wow
said Jane the puppy will weigh more than I do!

_____

_____

_____

_____

_____

_____

_____

_____

Rehoboth Beach
Rehoboth Beach is a little town on the Atlantic Ocean it is in the state
of Delaware Rehoboth is a popular summer resort people go there to
swim, boat, sunbathe, and fish there is a small boardwalk where
people like to walk at night.

_____

_____

_____

_____

_____

_____

Repairing Sentence Fragments

A sentence fragment is a part of a sentence. It is a group of words that
do not express a complete idea.

Sentence — I just got a new computer.

Fragment — Great machine!

Directions: • Read each group of words.
• Decide whether it is a sentence or a fragment.
• Write *Sentence* or *Fragment* on the line before each sentence.
• Rewrite each fragment into a complete sentence.

_____ **1)** My new computer not so expensive.

_____

_____ **2)** It does so much work for me.

_____

_____ **3)** The computer was a birthday present.

_____

_____ **4)** From my father, mother, and grandparents.

_____

_____ **5)** Word processing, the main use I expect to have for the computer.

_____

_____

_____ **6)** Word processing also called electronic typesetting.

_____

_____ **7)** Also, the computer would balance my checkbook.

_____

_____ **8)** If I had a checkbook, that is!

_____

_____ **9)** Of course, I bought a game or two.

_____

_____ **10)** Looking forward to playing them right after I finish my homework.

_____

_____

Writing Complete Sentences

Two common writing mistakes are the run-on sentence and the
sentence fragment.

A FRAGMENT is a part of sentence.

A RUN-ON is two or more sentences run together.

Directions: • Read each group of words.
• Identify the words as either a *fragment* or a *run-on*.
• Correct the mistake. Write the corrected sentence or
  sentences. You may need to add information.

EXAMPLE	*Run-on*	Thanksgiving is my favorite holiday I love to eat.

Thanksgiving is my favorite holiday because I love to eat.

---

1) _____ We watch the Super Bowl
it's the best game of the year.

_____

_____

2) _____ Last year skiing, next year
ice skating.

_____

_____

3) _____ What's your favorite sport,
mine's hockey.

_____

_____

4) _____ Rain, wind, lightning, and
thunder for hours.

_____

_____

5) _____ Under the chair the dog.

_____

_____

6) _____ In Florida and California
sunny skies.

_____

_____

7) _____ Taxes, taxes, and more taxes!

_____

_____

8) _____ The weather was pleasant
we enjoyed the day.

_____

_____

9) _____ What's BASIC, it's a
computer programming language.

_____

_____

10) _____ A complete sentence is
best, don't you agree?

_____

_____

Improving Sentences

A. Directions: • Improve these sentences.
              • The word in bold print is vague.
              • Choose a better word.
              • Write the new sentence below the old one.

1) Joseph thought that *Star Wars* was **exciting**.

_____

2) Ray **thought** the movie was **interesting**.

_____

3) A dictionary is a **nice** book to have.

_____

4) My! That building is **big**!

_____

5) Pie and ice cream make a **nice** dessert.

_____

B. Directions: • Improve these sentences.
              • Add either adjectives or adverbs.
              • Write the improved sentence.

EXAMPLE	The family went on vacation.
	***Recently** the **entire Marmo** family went on a **long** vacation.*

1) The teacher told the students about a book.

_____

2) A chipmunk was on my porch.

_____

3) Our neighbors bought a car.

_____

4) Cecilia is a friend of mine.

_____

5) Has anyone seen Harold?

_____

Combining Short Sentences

Directions: Combine these sentences.

1) A dog is an animal. A cat is an animal. A horse is an animal.

_____

_____

2) Last winter there was snow. Last winter there was sleet.

_____

_____

3) Frank walked to school. His brother walked to school.

_____

_____

4) Rob is a baker. Lee is a baker. The bakery is on Chester Avenue.

_____

_____

5) John filled out an application. The application was long. The application was complicated.

_____

_____

_____

6) Betty was interviewed. The interview was for a job. Betty was twenty years old.

_____

_____

_____

7) The girl is young. The girl is named Joan. The girl goes to school.

_____

_____

8) Rob is going to the concert. David is going to the concert. Frank isn't.

_____

_____

_____

9) Schools were closed. There had been a blizzard.

_____

_____

10) Bill was jogging. He fell. He hurt his knee. He hurt his ankle.

_____

_____

11) The family was on vacation. They went to Maine. They stayed for two weeks.

_____

_____

12) Chris goes to college. The college is large. The college is in Virginia. Chris is studying medicine.

_____

_____

_____

Connecting With Semicolons

You can use a semicolon (;) to connect sentences with the words listed below. Put a comma after the conjunction.

besides	furthermore	also	nevertheless
accordingly	otherwise	instead	therefore
moreover	however	then	consequently

EXAMPLE   Jack burned the cake; **therefore**, we had no dessert.
Semicolon + Conjunction + Comma

A. Directions: Punctuate these sentences correctly.

1) Pick up your room otherwise you will be in big trouble.

2) You want to be a star therefore you must practice.

3) We exercised for an hour then we rested.

4) We enjoy exercise moreover it makes us feel better.

5) Allen ate too much consequently he had indigestion.

B. Directions: Connect each pair of sentences using one of the conjunctions listed above. Punctuate each sentence correctly.

1) I like to swim in warm weather. Today is cold.

_____

_____

_____

2) We worked all day. We got the job done.

_____

_____

3) Kenny would like to be an engineer. He would also like to be an architect.

_____

_____

_____

4) Joan wants a Gold Medal. She practices many hours a day.

_____

_____

_____

5) Class began at 9 o'clock. The teacher expected the students to be there on time.

_____

_____

_____

Sentences to Improve

A. Directions: · Add at least one prepositional phrase to each sentence
below. Write the new sentence.

| EXAMPLE |

My friend went out.

*My friend **from Knoxville** went out **for a walk**.*

1) Everyone was out.

_____

2) The kitten looks sad.

_____

3) The team got three new players.

_____

4) The winters are cold here.

_____

5) Marlene is hungry.

_____

B. Directions: · Combine each pair of sentences below.
· Add a conjunction. Write the new sentence.

| EXAMPLE |

There was finally enough snow. We went skiing.

*There was finally enough snow, **so** we went skiing.*

1) We like the beach. We go there every summer.

_____

2) Jackie's Uncle has a farm. She goes horseback riding.

_____

3) Sometimes there is nothing to do. I just go for a walk.

_____

4) The city streets are noisy. They are also exciting.

_____

5) Dena got tickets for the concert. Karl got tickets for the concert.

_____

Punctuating With Subordinating Conjunctions

If you begin a sentence with a dependent clause, set it off with a comma.

When Alice graduated from high school, she received a diploma.

If you use the dependent clause after the independent clause, do not use a comma.

Alice received a diploma when she graduated from high school.

A. Directions: • Underline the dependent clause in each sentence.
• Add the correct punctuation.

1) If Dana has a chance he will go to summer camp.

2) While he is there he will earn money as a counselor.

3) Although Dana will be busy he will find time for recreation himself.

4) He plans to swim every day after he finishes his chores.

5) Because he likes kids and the great outdoors Dana always enjoys camp.

B. Directions: Combine each pair of the following sentences using one of these subordinating conjunctions: *after, although, because, if, unless, when,* and *while.* Write each sentence on the line. Add the correct punctuation.

1) The storm was over. We went outside.

_____

2) Dinner is ready. We can eat.

_____

3) Camp is over. We will write letters to our new friends.

_____

4) The tennis shoes are worn out. Cathy got new ones.

_____

5) We plan to visit Disney World. We are in Florida.

_____

Basic English Composition

Choosing a Topic Sentence

Directions: Choose the better topic sentence in each pair. Place a
check mark (✔) on the line before your answer.

1) _____ **A)** There are many interesting facts about ducks.

   _____ **B)** Ducks are animals that fly.

2) _____ **A)** Chairs, tables, and desks are furniture.

   _____ **B)** There is a wide variety of furniture.

3) _____ **A)** The encyclopedia can be used a lot.

   _____ **B)** The encyclopedia is a valuable book.

4) _____ **A)** The police force has a variety of responsibilities.

   _____ **B)** This paragraph will be about the police force.

5) _____ **A)** There are many fascinating careers.

   _____ **B)** There are many good jobs.

6) _____ **A)** Fashion designs change frequently.

   _____ **B)** Fashion designs change every season.

7) _____ **A)** Swimming is primarily a summer sport.

   _____ **B)** Swimming is a sport.

8) _____ **A)** The newspaper has information.

   _____ **B)** The newspaper is an information source.

9) _____ **A)** My favorite soap opera is "Another World."

   _____ **B)** There are many soap operas on TV.

10) _____ **A)** There is a variety of animals at the zoo.

   _____ **B)** I saw elephants, seals, polar bears, and ducks at the zoo.

Does It Belong?

Directions: Find the sentence that does not fit in the body of the paragraph. Underline it.

1) It was a beautiful day for sailing. Joe decided to take his sailboat out on the lake. He sailed for an hour. Joe had homework to do. He passed several other sailboats while on the lake.

2) Exercise is important. It keeps your body healthy. Reading is an enjoyable hobby. Jogging and swimming are excellent forms of exercise. There are other effective forms of exercise.

3) The children wanted a pet. The children wanted new bicycles. Their mother said they could have a puppy or a kitten if they promised to take care of it. They promised they would care for it and then asked for a puppy.

4) Robert enjoys driving. He likes sports cars. Robert prefers sports cars with convertible tops. He also prefers sports cars that are either blue or green. If he ever gets a sports car, he wants one with a five-speed transmission.

5) David and Fran went to the zoo. They saw elephants and seals. They saw a polar bear swimming. David watched the ducks eat, and Fran saw the baby donkey get a bath. The zoo was crowded.

6) Cake decorating is a time-consuming job. The icing must be the right consistency. Then you must add a small amount of coloring to a small amount of icing. This must be done for each different color used. Everyone will enjoy the cake. Then, using your colored icing, you decorate the cake with the picture or words wanted.

7) Choosing a career is difficult, but not impossible. Try to choose a career that you are good at and will enjoy. Education is important. Salary may be a factor when choosing a career, but it probably will not be the deciding factor.

8) The train is a form of transportation. It travels by land. The train can take you places much faster than a car. An airplane travels by air.

9) Eggs are an important food. They provide a great deal of needed protein. Meat provides protein. Eggs can be eaten at any meal and cooked in a variety of ways.

10) Space exploration is very important to the United States. It allows the country to explore other planets. Space exploration also enables this country to set up space satellites for world communication. Mexico is not involved in space exploration. The United States has launched many space missions.

Building a Paragraph With Facts

A paragraph is a group of sentences. We build a paragraph with information.

Directions: • Use the facts below to develop a paragraph that supports the topic sentence.
• Change the words around if you need to.
• Replace nouns with pronouns.
• Do not use facts that do not support the main idea.

Softball Facts
• The players swing a bat and try to hit a ball.
• When they get a hit, they run the bases.
• A softball team learns to work together.
• Sometimes, players need to slide into the base.
• After the game, everyone sits around talking.
• They run in the field to catch a fly ball.
• A game lasts about an hour.
• All players throw the ball around.

Softball is good exercise. _____

_____

_____

_____

_____

_____

_____

_____

_____

_____

Good Endings

Directions: Check the better conclusion for each paragraph.

1) It is important to choose safe toys for children. Toys that are sharp or too small are not appropriate for babies or small children. Toys for older children must be able to provide hours of entertainment.

_____ **a)** Books for children are also needed.
_____ **b)** Well-chosen toys will only benefit your children.

2) Beginning swimmers are required to develop a variety of skills. Each skill encourages the swimmer to be comfortable in the water by building a swimmer's confidence.

_____ **a)** Beginning swimmers are not expected to know every swimming stroke.
_____ **b)** A swimmer's confidence will enable him or her to learn any swimming stroke.

3) There are many kinds of television game shows. While the shows are different, they all give away money, prizes, or both. The people who try to win are called contestants.

_____ **a)** On these shows contestants are required to answer questions or do certain tasks before winning.
_____ **b)** It is fun to win.

4) Presenting the right image at a job interview is extremely important. Your appearance and manner of speech will affect the interviewer's opinion. The way in which you answer the questions will also affect your chances of being hired.

_____ **a)** Therefore, advance preparation is necessary for a successful interview.
_____ **b)** When you get the job, you can do what you want.

5) The telephone can be an important tool in an emergency. If someone is sick, in trouble, or injured, a phone call can save a life.

_____ **a)** Using the telephone to call an ambulance or the police is the fastest means of communication.
_____ **b)** It is also helpful to use a phone to communicate with friends.

6) Decoy carving is a craft begun many years ago. The original decoy carvers carved and painted very crude replicas of ducks. Today's decoy carvers are artists. They paint decoys that are almost lifelike.

_____ **a)** Decoys are used for hunting.
_____ **b)** However, the new decoy carvers based their decoys on the earlier versions.

Paragraph Writing Practice

Directions: • Use each group of sentences to build a paragraph.
                • The first sentence must express the main idea.
                • The body must support the main idea.
                • The last sentence must be a conclusion or a summary.

A. A Fire Protection Engineer

1) Builders consult these engineers to be sure the building follows the fire safety codes.
2) Most people have never heard of a fire protection engineer.
3) Communities hire fire protection engineers to decide where fire hydrants should be placed.
4) A fire protection engineer does an important job in a community.
5) After a fire, these engineers investigate to find out the cause.

_____

_____

_____

_____

_____

B. Being Letter Perfect

1) Are you neat or sloppy?
2) Every paper that you write in school says something more than words.
3) A reader can tell many things about a writer.
4) Are you careful or careless?
5) Do you think before you speak or write?
6) Your writing says something about you.

_____

_____

_____

_____

_____

Writing a Paragraph

A paragraph has three parts: a beginning, a middle, and an end.

Directions: • Follow the steps listed below.
                 • Write your own paragraph on a topic of your choice.
                 • Indent only the first sentence of the paragraph.
                 • Write an interesting title for the paragraph.

Step 1: The beginning of the paragraph is called the **topic sentence**. It states the main idea of a paragraph.
       Decide what subject you want to write about. Write a topic sentence that tells the reader what the paragraph is about.

Step 2: The middle of the paragraph is the **body**. The body tells about the subject. It has examples, details, and explanations.
       Write three or four sentences about the subject.

Step 3: The end of the paragraph is the **conclusion**. The last sentence of the paragraph should summarize the main idea.
       Write the conclusion to your paragraph.

Title _____

_____

_____

_____

_____

_____

_____

_____

_____

_____

_____

_____

Asking for Information

Directions: • Imagine that you are shopping for each of the items below.
• Write three specific questions that you would ask the
  salesperson about these items.
• Write your questions in complete sentences.

A. You are renting an apartment.

1) _____

2) _____

3) _____

B. You are buying a new car.

1) _____

2) _____

3) _____

C. You are selecting a new telephone.

1) _____

2) _____

3) _____

D. You are buying a puppy at a pet store.

1) _____

2) _____

3) _____

Chronologic Order

Chronologic order means order according to time.

Directions: • Put each set of facts in chronologic order. Number
the first event 1, the next event 2, and so forth.
• Use the facts to write a paragraph. Write a topic
sentence and a conclusion.

Topic I: History of Oregon

A) _____ Oregon entered the Union in 1859.

B) _____ In 1848, Oregon became a United States territory.

C) _____ Spanish seamen were the first Europeans to spot the Oregon coast.

D) _____ Oregon was a progressive state, giving women the right to vote in 1912.

E) _____ In 1975, Oregon became the first state to ban aerosol cans using fluorocarbons.

F) _____ The earliest known residents of Oregon were Indians.

Topic II: The Olympic Games

A) _____ The first Olympics had only one event—a 200-yard foot race.

B) _____ In 394 A.D., the Roman emperor banned the games.

C) _____ The first modern Olympic Games were held in Athens, Greece, in 1896.

D) _____ The first Olympic Games were held in Athens, Greece, in 776 B.C.

E) _____ Now, over 100 nations around the world participate.

Paragraph Purpose

Every paragraph has a purpose. Some reasons for writing a paragraph are:

A. To inform and explain   **D.** To ask for information
B. To tell how to do something   **E.** To persuade someone your idea is right
C. To tell a story

Directions: Read each of these paragraphs. Decide the purpose of each
one. Match each paragraph with the correct purpose from
the list given. Write the letter of the purpose on the line.

_____ **1)**   Dear Mary,
      I am writing to give you the directions to my house. Take
Route 450; then go east on Route 50 toward Annapolis. Go
ten miles. Then take Route 197 north. Turn right at the third
traffic light.
                 Your friend,
                 Ella Sue

_____ **2)**   Dear Mr. Franklin,
      I am writing to apply for the summer job you advertised in
the newspaper. My résumé is enclosed. I will call you on
Thursday to learn more about it.
                 Sincerely,
                 Robert Byers
                 Robert Byers

_____ **3)**   It was just about midnight. We heard a loud screeching
noise just outside our house. It was our neighbor on his
motorcycle. The whole family was suddenly awake. We
rushed to the window. Everyone breathed a sigh of relief
when the noise stopped.

_____ **4)**   A computer language is a special set of words or codes. The
computer understands these codes. For example, if you enter
one word or code, the computer knows it is supposed to open
a file. If you enter another word or code, the computer
prints a file.

Rewriting Topic Sentences

Directions: Improve these topic sentences.

1) You have to do things like practice and concentrate if you want to be good at baseball.

_____

_____

2) Novels that tell why people do things are good very often.

_____

_____

3) Old things that you can find in attics are interesting.

_____

_____

4) Different spices go into a lot of gourmet foods.

_____

_____

5) If one wants a good job then he should have skills for it.

_____

_____

6) Swimmers ought to know rules which will help them be safe.

_____

_____

7) If you want to enjoy something, look at a sunset.

_____

_____

8) Insects do things that human beings often do.

_____

_____

9) Children who watch television can have their attitudes influenced by television.

_____

_____

10) I know a guy named Charles who is always forgetting something.

_____

_____

11) There are things about tennis and baseball that are the same.

_____

_____

12) Even though Jill and Jean were twins, they were not the same.

_____

_____

13) There are a lot of things you can do with old newspapers.

_____

_____

14) Kittens can make you laugh with the things they do.

_____

_____

Transitional Words and Phrases

Directions: • Find 20 transitional words and phrases in the puzzle. The
words and phrases are across, down, diagonal, and
backwards.
• List them in the spaces below the puzzle.
• Use each one in a sentence.
• To review transitional words see textbook page 208.

```
I  F  E  T  R  F  A  S  A  R  E  S  U  L  T  U  Q
N  N  D  F  U  R  T  H  E  R  M  O  R  E  T  H  E
C  V  T  V  I  R  R  T  H  E  R  E  F  O  R  E  T
O  B  H  H  D  R  A  R  A  H  G  F  V  B  R  D  S
N  E  E  E  E  L  S  Q  W  W  O  A  A  A  N  N  A
C  C  Y  Y  Y  M  M  T  T  R  T  W  W  E  O  O  L
L  W  L  W  T  T  E  Z  X  V  B  Z  E  E  O  O  T
U  E  L  I  H  W  N  A  E  M  M  H  H  V  S  X  A
S  Q  A  Q  E  O  Q  L  N  N  T  T  E  N  E  R  R
I  N  N  R  W  W  Q  S  Q  T  H  P  R  N  N  R  W
O  O  I  I  E  F  Q  O  A  A  I  Q  O  G  L  L  Q
N  W  F  W  F  Z  I  X  X  T  X  M  F  T  H  E  N
D  Y  W  O  R  R  O  M  O  T  L  Q  E  E  X  Q  U
S  F  O  R  E  X  A  M  P  L  E  E  B  W  H  L  N
```

• Fill in these lines with your answers.

1) A _ _ _
2) A_ _ _ _ _ _ _ _
3) A_ _ _ _ _
4) A_ _ _ _ _ _ _
5) B_ _ _ _ _
6) F _ _ _ _ _ _
7) F _ _ _ _
8) F _ _ _ _ _ _ _ _
9) F _ _ _ _ _ _ _
10) H _ _ _ _ _ _

11) I_ _ _ _ _ _ _ _ _ _ _
12) I_ _ _ _ _ _ _ _ _ _ _
13) L _ _ _ _
14) M _ _ _ _ _ _ _ _
15) N _ _ _
16) N _ _
17) S _ _ _
18) T _ _ _
19) T _ _ _ _ _ _ _
20) T _ _ _ _ _ _ _

Using Transitional Words

Directions: Rewrite these paragraphs. Add some transitional words or phrases such as *then, first, meanwhile, later, next, before, finally, also.*

Anthony walked onto the tennis court. He was ready to serve. He tossed the ball into the air. He hit it hard. He really wanted to win the match.

_____

_____

_____

_____

_____

_____

Suzanne watched the waves coming in. She looked around for her parents. She saw them. She decided to hold their hands. The ocean looked too rough today.

_____

_____

_____

_____

_____

_____

Computers do many things to help us. They keep banking records. They do difficult problems in math. They even change traffic lights in big cities.

_____

_____

_____

_____

_____

_____

_____

_____

Pete studied the pitcher carefully. It was his turn to bat. A solid hit would bring in the winning run. He stepped up to the plate. His eyes followed the ball right until it met his bat. He knew he helped win the game.

_____

_____

_____

_____

_____

_____

_____

_____

Making Comparisons

Comparisons can make your ideas clearer. They can be direct or indirect.

Indirect: The baby's skin is **as smooth as silk.**

Direct: Judy is **a puzzle** to everyone

A. Directions: Underline the comparisons in the following sentences. Decide whether the comparisons are direct or indirect. Write *direct* or *indirect* on the line.

_____ **1)** That song is like a beautiful dream.

_____ **2)** That skyscraper looks like the Empire State Building.

_____ **3)** "Sally is a dream come true," sighed Roger.

_____ **4)** My dog is as brave as Lassie.

_____ **5)** Fred is as old as the hills.

_____ **6)** Dan is a mountain of a man.

B. Directions: Complete the statements below. Be creative!

1) A cup of coffee in the morning is a _____

_____

2) The sky grew as dark as _____

_____

3) Poetry is the _____

_____

4) The victory was like a _____

_____

5) Tomorrow will be as _____

_____

Improving a Paragraph

Directions: Read the following paragraph carefully. Proofread the paragraph for mistakes. Make corrections. Then write it correctly on the back of this paper or on your own paper.

For You to Do:

1) Improve the topic sentence.

2) Be sure the body supports the main idea.

3) Improve the summary sentence.

4) Add sentence variety and transitions.

5) Check for run-on sentences and fragments.

6) Check spelling. Correct any errors.

7) Check punctuation and capitalization.

8) Check verbs for errors.

Reference Sources

Do you know what reference sources are. They are books and also files that helps us to find lots of information. The library has most of them but cant be tooken home. A library catalog is a list of all books a library got. If you know the title and author you can find it easy. The dictionary atlas and encyclopedia are other reference books, maybe you never heard of *who's who in america.* it has names of famous people and tells about them. If you dont know what a thesaurus *Readers' Guide* and almanac is used for, you oughta find out, they can help with your schoolwork.

Proofreading Practice

Directions: • Read the paragraph below very carefully. Circle these
kinds of mistakes:
  Spelling
  Capitalization
  Punctuation
  Sentence errors
• Correct the mistakes.
• Rewrite the improved paragraph below.

Why I Quit Bowling

For many years, I enjoyed bowlling. Too year ago I quit my team and
this be the reason why. The name of my team were the starframers. A
starframe in bowlling means that everyone gots a spare or a strike in
that frame. We was great, everyones averages kept improving.
Naturally, we was in first place all year. Finally it was the last nite of
the season, my team had went into the final position round three
games ahead of the second place teem. Confidence was our middle
name that Night! We only had to win one game to take home the first
place trophy. All I can says is that I is looking right now at a second
place trophy. Yes, we lost all four games, surely, no more needs to
be said.

_____

_____

_____

_____

_____

_____

_____

_____

_____

_____

Identifying People, Places, and Things

To **identify** means to tell the most important characteristics about something.

Directions: • Identify each person, place, or thing.
• Write one complete sentence stating the characteristics that make them different or recognizable.
• Use a dictionary as needed.

1) Neapolitan ice cream _____

_____

_____

_____

2) Naugahyde _____

_____

_____

_____

3) haberdasher _____

_____

_____

_____

4) Winston Churchill _____

_____

_____

_____

5) Carson City _____

_____

_____

_____

6) Casablanca _____

_____

_____

_____

7) bighorn _____

_____

_____

_____

8) Thanksgiving _____

_____

_____

_____

9) rya rug _____

_____

_____

_____

10) trinket _____

_____

_____

_____

11) trilogy _____

_____

_____

_____

12) NATO _____

_____

_____

_____

Become an Essayist

An **essayist** is a person who writes essays. You can write excellent essays by remembering a few easy facts.

- Paragraphs are groups of sentences about a subject.
- A paragraph has three parts:
  1. a topic sentence
  2. a body
  3. a summary or conclusion
- Always proofread your work. Mechanics are important in helping you communicate your ideas.

Directions: Select one of the following topics, or make up one of your own. Write your first draft in the space provided. Proofread and revise your essay. Then write your final draft on a separate paper.

> **Topics:** A Typical Saturday at My House
>
> My Pick for This Year's Super Bowl Champs and Why
>
> The Funniest Things My Pet Ever Did
>
> The Most Beautiful Place in the World
>
> The Girl (Boy) Whom I'll Marry

First Draft

_____

_____

_____

_____

_____

_____

_____

_____

_____

_____

_____

Developing a Brief Essay From Facts

Directions: Write an essay response about each group of items below. Use the list of facts in each group.

Facts About the Mammoth

1. It no longer exists.
2. It was a large elephant-like animal.
3. It was about nine feet tall.
4. It had long curved tusks.
5. It is believed to have had hairy skin.

A) Describe the mammoth. Write your description here:

_____

_____

_____

_____

_____

_____

_____

_____

_____

Facts About Antarctica

1. It is a continent.
2. It is located around and near the South Pole.
3. It is about 5,000,000 square miles in size.
4. It is extremely cold there most of the year.
5. Very little life exists there.

B) Describe Antarctica. Write your description here:

_____

_____

_____

_____

_____

_____

_____

Facts About Mercury

1. It is the closest planet to the sun.
2. It has no moons.
3. It takes 58 earth days to rotate once on its axis.
4. It takes 88 earth days to make one trip around the sun.
5. It is only 36,000,000 miles from the sun.

C) Describe the planet Mercury. Write your description here:

_____

_____

_____

_____

_____

_____

_____

Leave a Message

Directions: • Read the following conversation.
• Write the message that Pete should leave for Audrey.
• Use today's date and the current time.

Audrey was out on a job. She repairs television sets for a living. Pete is her husband. He teaches science at the high school.

When Pete got home from school, the telephone was ringing.

"Hello," he said. "Haswell TV repairs."

"Hello," the voice on the phone said. "My television is broken and we wanted to watch a special program tonight. Can Mrs. Haswell get over right away?"

"I'll give her the message. Give me your name, address, and telephone and number."

"OK. My name is Dana Kurtz. I live at 4320 Foxhill Drive. My phone number is 555-1298. Tell her it's an emergency."

"I will. Thanks for calling, Miss Kurtz. Good-bye."

"Good-bye."

After he hung up the telephone, Pete wrote the message on the memo pad below.

To _____

Date _____ **Time** _____

WHILE YOU WERE OUT

M _____

of _____

Phone No. _____

TELEPHONED		PLEASE CALL	
WAS IN TO SEE YOU		WILL CALL BACK	
WANTS TO SEE YOU		**URGENT**	
RETURNED YOUR CALL			

MESSAGE _____

_____

_____

_____

_____

_____

_____

_____

More About Memos

Directions: Write a memo to a friend in your class. Ask the friend about a homework assignment.

Directions: Write a memo to a family member. Tell the family member what you want for your birthday.

MEMO

Date: _____

To: _____

From: _____

Subject: _____

_____

_____

_____

_____

_____

_____

_____

MEMO

Date: _____

To: _____

From: _____

Subject: _____

_____

_____

_____

_____

_____

_____

_____

Writing Memos

Directions: • Read the letters below.
  • Rewrite each one into memo form.
  • Use the current year.

October 4, 20 _____

Dear Mrs. Wilson,

   Please excuse Frankie Neal's absence from school last Friday. Frankie had the flu.

              Sincerely,

              Mrs. D. Neal

              Mrs. D. Neal

April 19, 20 _____

Dear Mr. Howard,

   The girls in the seventh grade would like to have a tennis team. Would you help us make the arrangements?
   Thank you very much.

              Sincerely,

              Rae Caldwell

              Rae Caldwell, Secretary
              Seventh Grade Girls

```
        MEMO
Date: _____
To: _____
From: _____
Subject: _____
_____
_____
_____
_____
_____
_____
_____
```

```
        MEMO
Date: _____
To: _____
From: _____
Subject: _____
_____
_____
_____
_____
_____
_____
_____
_____
```

Preparing a Memo

Directions: Read the following notice. Review it for any missing
important details. Then with the important information
included, rewrite it as a memo on the lines provided below.
Use today's date.

ATTENTION

Beginning tomorrow and for the next two days, Central High School will
be holding auditions for its annual Student-Faculty Talent Show. If you
sing, dance, play a musical instrument, do stand-up comedy, read poetry
with real feeling, or in any other way can keep an audience entertained
for several minutes, then you are the kind of person we need. Take that
first small step to the stars and show us what you can do. Our talent
committee is ready to select. We look forward to seeing your act. For
further information, contact anyone on the talent committee. Good luck!

Committee Chairperson

_____

_____

_____

_____

_____

_____

_____

_____

_____

_____

_____

_____

_____

_____

_____

Addressing an Envelope

Addressing an envelope correctly is important. If we go to the trouble of writing a letter, we want to be sure it gets to the right place.

Return Address →
Christy Walker
3212 Harrigut Avenue, Apt. 201
Dayton, OH 45442

Mailing Address →
Ms. Bland Pearson
23 Tralee Way
San Rafael, CA 94903

Directions: • Below are some sample addresses. They are all wrong in some way.
• Rewrite them correctly.
• Use the examples above as a guide.

1) Tony Pierce
Dartmouth Ct 17
Trenton, NJ 08601

_____

_____

_____

2) Janet Lahney
Apt. 13
92 Westland Drive
College Park, MD 20740

_____

_____

_____

3) Valerie Armstrong
67 Tulip Drive
19050 Lansdowne, PA

_____

_____

_____

4) Marty Jo Golato
Sartoga avenue 4210
95129
CA San Jose

_____

_____

_____

5) taffy clayton
Cumberland MD 21502
517 Louisville Lane

_____

_____

_____

6) Jill Edmonds
43 main street apt 101
Poughkeepsie NY 12603

_____

_____

_____

Label the Parts of a Letter

Directions: Choose the words from the box that match with the parts of the following letter. Write the correct name of each part on the line beside that part.

Closing	Body	Date
Signature	Name	Return Address
Inside Address	Greeting	Addressee

2712 Filbert Lane
Brownsville, USA 73501   } _____

March 12, 20 _____   _____

Mark Casso
321 Knowledge Drive   _____
Lubbock, Texas 79408   } _____

Dear Mr. Casso: _____

    I heard that you were looking for an associate for your law firm. I am a recent law school graduate. My résumé is enclosed for your review.

    April 12-15 I will be visiting Lubbock on other business. If possible, I would like to have an interview with you at that time. I will call you on March 15 to talk with you about this.   } _____

        Sincerely yours,

        Mary Stein   _____
        Mary Stein   _____

Edit Your Letters

Directions: Read the following letter carefully. Circle all the mistakes that you find. Then rewrite the letter correctly. Look for spelling, punctuation, capitalization, form, and other kinds of mistakes.

Richard Kochert
3412 wilson avenue
Anderson IN
46011

August 12, 20 ____
mr. Harold sweet
1111 Albany bvd.
anderson, IN 46011

Dear harold:

    I am writing in response to your advertisement in the *Anderson Daily Blade*. I am interested in the managment trainee position that you described. I am enclosing my résumé fer you're information. I am available to begin work immediately.

    I will call you for an interview on Wednesday morning.

very sincerely yours

Richard Kochert

Richard Kochert

_____

_____

_____

_____

_____

_____

_____

_____

_____

_____

_____

_____

_____

_____

Understanding the Letter

Directions: In the space provided, answer each question or complete each direction.

1) Name the two basic kinds of letters.

   a) _____

   b) _____

2) Which kind of letter is considered formal?

   _____

3) Which kind of letter is considered informal?

   _____

4) Name the basic parts of a business letter.

   a) _____

   b) _____

   c) _____

   d) _____

   e) _____

   f) _____

   g) _____

   h) _____

5) Does a business letter have an inside address?

   _____

6) Would a personal letter be written in block form?

   _____

7) What is another word for "salutation"?

   _____

8) Name the part of the letter in which a person states what he or she wants to say.

   _____

9) In a personal letter, which punctuation mark follows the salutation?

   _____

10) In a business letter, which punctuation mark follows the salutation?

   _____

11) What kind of letter would have this closing—*Very truly yours*?

   _____

12) What punctuation mark follows the closing of a letter?

   _____

13) Write today's date. Punctuate it correctly.

   _____

14) Rewrite this address correctly:
Madden, Mary Dr.
Lyndhurst, N.J.
41 Rutland Road
07032

   _____

   _____

   _____

Library Catalog Entries

The catalog in a library lists every book the library has. Books have
three types of records: title, author, subject.

Directions: • Put the list below in alphabetic order the way each
entry would be in a library catalog.
• Identify each one as a subject, an author, or a title.

John Steinbeck	*The Writer's Handbook*	history
Olympics, history	Pearl Buck	*The Red Pony*
Gone With the Wind	William Shakespeare	*Hamlet*
Russia	psychology	S. E. Hinton
Joyce Carol Oates	*The Outsiders*	art

List the entries here.   Identify each one here.

1) _____   _____

2) _____   _____

3) _____   _____

4) _____   _____

5) _____   _____

6) _____   _____

7) _____   _____

8) _____   _____

9) _____   _____

10) _____   _____

11) _____   _____

12) _____   _____

13) _____   _____

14) _____   _____

15) _____   _____

Report Acrostic

Directions: Read each clue. Fill in the blanks with the letters of the
words that match each clue. Then solve the acrostic puzzle.

1) A book with information __ __ __ __ __ __ __ __ __
                               3 6 8 6 3 6 10 1 6

2) A book of maps __ __ __ __ __
                       2 7 4 2 15

3) A book about famous people __ __ __ ' __ __ __ __
                                   5 16 9 15 5 16 9

4) Published at regular intervals __ __ __ __ __ __ __ __ __ __
                                       11 6 3 12 9 14 12 1 2 4

5) It lists articles from
magazines __ __ __ __ __ __ __ ' __ __ __ __ __
           3 6 2 14 6 3 15 13 17 12 14 6

6) A period of time __ __ __ __
                         7 6 3 18

7) A list of topics in a book __ __ __ __ __
                                   12 10 14 6 19

8) According to time __ __ __ __ __ __ __ __ __ __ __
                          1 16 3 9 10 9 4 9 13 12 1

9) A list of books __ __ __ __ __ __ __ __ __ __ __ __
                        20 12 20 4 12 9 13 3 2 11 16 21

10) An error __ __ __ __ __ __ __
                  18 12 15 7 2 22 6

Acrostic Puzzle

__ __ __ __ __ __ __ __ __
7 16 6 22 6 21 7 9 2

__ __ __ __ __ __ __ __ __ __
15 17 1 1 6 15 15 8 17 4

__ __ __ __ __ __ __ __ __ __ __ __ __ __ __
3 6 11 9 3 7 12 15 11 4 2 10 10 12 10 13

Writing an Outline

Directions: • Look at Outline A. Use it as a guide.
• Rewrite Outline B on your writing paper. Punctuate the outline correctly. Indent the lines correctly. Capitalize the first word of each topic. Capitalize proper nouns.

Outline A

Cyprus

I. Introduction
   A. Location
   B. Size
      1. Area
      2. Population
II. Geographical features
   A. Mountains
   B. Rivers
III. Political features
   A. Capital city
   B. Other large cities
IV. Agriculture and industry
   A. Crops
      1. Fruits
      2. Vegetables
   B. Minerals
      1. Copper
      2. Asbestos
V. Summary
   A. Important facts
   B. Conclusions

Outline B

United States History

I   Introduction
II   The discovery of America
      a   early Spanish explorers
      B The first permanent settlements
3   The colonial period
      A Early governments
      b Indian relations
4   The Revolutionary Period
      A. Important leaders
      B Important battles
V.   Forming a government
      A. The Articles of confederation
      B. The Constitution
      C. influences of early presidents
         1. George Washington
      2. Thomas Jefferson
Vi Summary and conclusions

Organizing Topics for an Outline

Directions: Put each set of topics below together in a logical order
to make an outline. Be sure to use correct punctuation.

Step 1: Identify the main topics.
Step 2: Identify the subtopics that belong with each main topic.

Sports Around the Word

Baseball   _____

Soccer   _____

Basketball   _____

Tennis   _____

Outdoor Sports   _____

Indoor Sports   _____

Volleyball   _____

Ice Hockey   _____

Football   _____

A Typical Daily Menu

Eggs and Bacon   _____

Soup   _____

Toast   _____

Dinner   _____

Sandwich   _____

Breakfast   _____

Entree (Main Dish)   _____

Vegetable   _____

Salad   _____

Beverage   _____

Fruit Juice   _____

Cereal and Milk   _____

Lunch   _____

Milk   _____

Dessert   _____

Preparing a Bibliography

Directions: • Prepare a bibliography using the facts below in
alphabetic order by the author's last name.
• If no author is identified, use the title.
• Put each set of facts into the correct form. Use the
example below.
• Be sure to indent in reverse as the sample shows.

EXAMPLE   Pettis, A.M. <u>Basic Car Care</u>. N.Y.: Simon &
Schuster, 1998.

---

1) Michael Bannigan's book called <u>Using a Video Camera</u>. Published
in 1995 in Washington, DC by Wilson Books, Inc.

_____

_____

2) <u>Operating a Television Station</u> by Vic Gamble. Published in
Boston in 1996 by Video Productions Publications.

_____

_____

3) "Writing a Television Play" by Ellen Stein in <u>Video Producer's
Magazine</u>, Volume 3. Published in November 1997 on
pages 56-76.

_____

_____

4) <u>The History of Television</u> by Collette Legarette. Published by
BCTV Publishing Company, 1995, in Seattle.

_____

_____

5) "Audio" in the 1994 <u>Television Encyclopedia</u>, Vol. 11,
pages 231-235. (No author given)

_____

_____